How, How the Carabao

Tales of Teaching English in the Philippines

How, How the Carabao

Tales of Teaching English in the Philippines

Isabel Pefianco Martin

EDITOR

PUBLISHED BY ATENEO DE MANILA UNIVERSITY LOYOLA SCHOOLS

The National Library of the Philippines CIP Data

Recommended entry:

    How, how the carabao : tales of teaching
        English in the Philippines / edited by
        Isabel Pefianco Martin. – Quezon
        City : Ateneo de Manila University,
        c2009.
                p. ; cm.

        1. Teachers' writings, Philippine.
    2. English language–Study and teaching.
    3. Philippine essays.   I. Martin, Isabel Pefianco.

PL6058.8   899.2104008'0921'3711   2009   P094000086
ISBN 978-971-0426-09-6

Distributed by
ATENEO DE MANILA UNIVERSITY PRESS
Bellarmine Hall, ADMU Campus
Katipunan Ave., Loyola Heights, Quezon City
P.O. Box 154, 1099 Manila, Philippines
Tel.: (632) 426-59-84 / Fax: (632) 426-59-09
Email: unipress@admu.edu.ph
Website: www.ateneopress.org

Contents

Preface

The events of the year 2009 remind us of our commitment as we celebrate the Sesquicentennial of the Ateneo de Manila University—to help build the nation amidst adversities that have affected countless Filipinos: the global financial crisis, hostage crises in the south, the A H1N1 flu scare, the passing of President Corazon Aquino, the onslaught of typhoons Ondoy and Pepeng and the accompanying floods. At the cusp of the national election in 2010, our country continues to be predominantly poor, its complex culture challenged, and its governance largely ineffectual. Yet, despite seemingly grim prospects, everywhere there are signs and examples of heroism, resilience, and transformation in our communities, leaders, and young people. There is hope.

It is in this desire to frame the events and problems that beset our country from a positive and hopeful perspective that the Loyola Schools has put together an *Agenda for Hope,* one that would be the Loyola Schools scholarly work contribution to national development on the occasion of the 150th anniversary of the Ateneo de Manila University.

What kind of scholarly work would help move the country forward and give our people hope? After several rounds of discussions with various faculty members and University leaders, we agreed on five key areas of engagement where we could realistically produce change within our lifetime. These would be our Agenda for Hope:

- to share prosperity
- to democratize governance
- to promote sustainable development
- to transform and preserve Philippine identity and culture
- to inspire our youth

Five groups were formed, composed of more than forty faculty members representing twenty or so disciplines. Scholars from such fields as philosophy, political science, chemistry, sociology, biology, economics, management, literature, psychology, theology, mathematics, and English, brought their research and expertise to bear in addressing the five points of the agenda. Providing a diverse range of perspectives, the authors offer ideas that are realistic, feasible, propose new directions for the future, motivate the audience into engagement and action, and reflect the Ateneo thinking and way of doing things.

Their works now comprise the seeds of the *Agenda for Hope*, which can be sown and spread to get others engaged in this effort to help build a nation. Create a government truly concerned for its constituents. Evolve a society with an improved quality of life. Weave a culture with the knowledge and depth of identity. Nurture an environment for future generations. Transform a people who will bring about these changes.

We thank Dr. Anna Miren Gonzalez-Intal, the first Vice President for the Loyola Schools, who, together with the Deans, originated the idea of an Agenda for Hope. We acknowledge and thank the coordinators of the five groups: Rev. Fr. Jose Magadia, S.J., Dr. Cristina Montiel, Dr. Czarina Saloma-Akpedonu, Dr. Remmon Barbaza, Dr. Fabian Dayrit, Dr. Fernando Aldaba, Dr. Ma. Emma Concepcion Liwag, and Dr. Liane Peña Alampay. We also thank the authors and editors, and the reviewers and members of the Loyola Schools community who provided feedback in preliminary presentations of the papers.

We look forward to the fruits that this *Agenda for Hope* will bear.

MARIA ASSUNTA C. CUYEGKENG, PH.D.
Vice President for the Loyola Schools
07 October 2009

In Admiration and Awe
AN INTRODUCTION TO THE ANTHOLOGY

ISABEL PEFIANCO MARTIN
Ateneo de Manila University

Pen pen de sarapen
De kutsilyo de almasen
Haw haw de karabaw batutin

Any Filipino child who has played in the streets should be familiar with *Pen Pen de Sarapen*. It is a children's song that has found its way to popular poems and OPM songs, such as Eraserhead's *Toyang*. One line from that children's song, "Haw haw de karabaw," has been used to refer to the so-called "carabao English," a language that educated Filipinos often hold with disdain. This is the language that is frequently ridiculed and looked down upon. This is the language that English teachers in the Philippines desperately try to remedy.

In choosing *How, How the Carabao* as the title of this book, I do not wish to present a negative image of carabao English, nor of Filipino teachers and learners of the language. On the contrary, this collection of tales about teaching English in the Philippines is an attempt to celebrate the heroism of Filipino teachers in the public schools. I have been teaching English for twenty years at the Ateneo de Manila University. During these wonderful years, I have come to realize that my experiences, especially the many challenges I face daily as an English teacher, pale in comparison to the colorful and sometimes absurd experiences of my counterparts in the public schools. Public school teachers of English are heroes. And this anthology is a tribute to their courage and resolve.

English language teaching (ELT) in the Philippines, especially where the public school system is concerned, is an undertaking largely relegated to the margins. The basic education sector is perceived to be a neglected and vertically structured monolith where everything—from policy to budget to curriculum to teacher training—is decided from the distant political center. One does not expect the system to be efficient and productive. However, an up-close look, belies this perception. Within that monolith are inspiring stories of victory and triumph.

For this collection of stories about ELT in the public schools, a Call for Contributions was circulated through DepEd Memorandum No. 165 Series 2008. Of twenty submissions, only twelve stories by public school teachers of English were selected for inclusion in this anthology. These twelve stories represent the twelve funniest, most touching, and most inspiring real-life stories about teaching English in the public schools.

The anthology has two sections. The first section is a collection of stories that draw attention to the challenges of teaching in the public schools. Because English in not native to most Filipinos, teaching the language in the Philippines is a difficult task. It is doubly difficult when one is assigned to teach English in the public schools where the language, as well as the resources necessary for effective ELT, is not as accessible as it is in the political and economic centers.

In the first story, Rebecca G. Magdirila of Balatong Elementary School (Laoag City) writes about how she morphed from being silent and shy to being the funny and boisterous teacher she has become. As her classroom was always noisy and the students always active, Ms. Magdirila learned to "relish every moment—whether quiet or chaotic, disciplined or unruly." After all, every moment with her students was a transformative and meaningful experience.

In "The Tough Get Going," Marilyn C. Braganza of Baguio National School of Arts and Trades (Davao City) narrates how her students try very hard, despite their poverty, to get to school in order to study their lessons. In declaring war against ignorance, Ms. Braganza spent her own hard-earned pesos to reproduce reading texts for the students who forced themselves to read. Ms. Braganza writes: "Teaching English in a public school is indeed sacrifice and joy rolled into one. The task is definitely difficult, but I am having fun. And my students are my greatest rewards."

Desiree Calvero Hidalgo of Urdaneta City National High School (Pangasinan), in her story "To Do the Best Until the End," talks about how the low points in her teaching pushed her to take a job at a bank. But she soon found herself back in the classroom, as she could not cut off the "invisible string that connected me to my young wards." Ms. Hidalgo writes about missing "the shared laughter, the wide-eyed innocence, even their impertinence and irreverence."

In the story "The Red Carabao," Dionisia B. Fernandez of Salomague Norte Elementary School (Pangasinan) laments the perceived deterioration in learning often associated with the public school system. Ms. Fernandez believes that public school teachers are partly to blame, and yet, these same teachers can do something to make a change. In her story, Ms. Fernandez shares her experiences with naughty Juan, who inspired her to formulate creative ways of teaching English to her students.

In "Hello, Miss Slow Down…," Shirley Jean V. Sugano of Macopa Elementary School (Compostela Valley), talks about how her own experience of learning to read enriches her teaching of reading. Ms. Sugano writes: "Elementary school children are notoriously unpredictable so teachers must expect the unexpected." Ms. Sugano compares the art of teaching to farming, which requires much patience in sowing seeds, applying fertilizers, and watering plants until they grow fully.

An English teacher is not just a teacher, as Marissa L. Arambulo of Santa Rosa Elementary School Central I (Laguna) relates in "An English Teacher Wears Many Hats." Ms. Arambulo comes from a family of teachers and so she is familiar with all the constraints and challenges of the profession. She writes about how she has become a mother, friend, companion, critic, coach, adviser, and guidance counselor to her students.

The teaching profession is not for the faint-hearted. When faced with trials and adversities, the teacher responds, not with tolerance, but with creativity. Mariam B. Rivamonte of Santa Cruz Central School (Marinduque), in her story "Excuse me Ma'am, what's the English word for…," talks about how she survives by practicing reflective teaching. She writes: "In the Philippines, teachers of English really need to be patient. We need to burn our eyebrows and think of creative solutions to help our students become good speakers of English. Instant remedies do not work—only gradual, step-by-step strategies do."

The second section of this anthology presents stories about the rewards of teaching English in the public schools. These teaching tales are sources of inspiration as the teachers narrate how they themselves learn from their students.

In "My English Teaching Journey," Maria Villamin Pineda of Marinduque National High School (Isok Boac, Marinduque) likens her teaching to sea-travel from one port to another in Lucena. She writes: "Like the sea, each school year is filled with unpredictable events, from the very smooth to the very rough conditions that may wreck boats." Ms. Pineda narrates how she was inspired by her readings to travel to Europe, especially to Venice, which she had always dreamed of visiting. The trip enriched her teaching tremendously. As she now faces retirement, Ms. Pineda dreams of reading stories to her grandchildren.

In "The Ways I love Thee," Rhea Christina U. Rabin of San Pablo City Science High School (Laguna) narrates how she expresses different ways of loving her students. Following Elizabeth Barrett Browning's poem "How do I Love Thee," Ms. Rabin speaks the ways, listens to the ways, reads the ways, and writes the ways of love. She ends her story with thank you notes and love letters from students who have long left her English classroom.

In the next story "Elmo and English Time," Hipolito M. Berano of Cajidiocan National High School (Romblon) shares his experiences with Elmo, a high school student who helped him compose a song about how wonderful English time is. Mr. Berano is an Inland Fisheries major who found himself teaching English soon after he had graduated from college. Now a school principal, Mr. Berano looks back at the meaningful and unforgettable encounters he had with his students when he was an English teacher.

Apolonia Marites O. Hernandez, now of Sto. Niño National High School (Batangas City), used to take a boat every week to get to a public school located on an island far from her sick mother. In that school, Ms. Hernandez spent countless hours of special reading sessions with students who were slow in reading. Dyna was one of them. In the story "Dining with Dyna," Ms. Hernandez relates how her efforts at teaching reading were rewarded as Dyna had become a successful professional with a bright future.

This collection of tales about teaching English culminates in the story "Never Give Up on Geoffrey." Lito A. Palomar of Antipolo National High School (Antipolo City) writes about how his student Geoffrey made great sacrifices so that he could complete his homework assignments in English. Mr. Palomar had taken financially rewarding jobs before deciding to teach. But only the teaching profession offered "the satisfaction of the heart and definition of the soul." His story is an inspiring account of how a simple thesaurus has changed the lives of an English teacher and his student.

After teaching English for many years—in my case, for twenty long years—one is tempted to believe that one has seen it all. Not true! These twelve tales of teaching English in the public schools offer rich experiences and fresh insights that are not apparent to those of us who thrive in the comforts of the private sector. From Laoag City up north, to the Compostela Valley down south, from the nearby mountains of Antipolo City, to the far-flung island province of Marinduque, each tale of teaching is a testament to the daily struggles public school teachers of English face. One can only marvel at their heroism and regard these teachers with admiration and awe.

HOW, HOW THE CARABAO

The Challenges of Teaching English

Growing in English

REBECCA G. MAGDIRILA
Balatong Elementary School, Laoag City

I was a woman of few words when I first became a teacher. I was in fact often tagged as a silent worker in my community. But when I became a teacher and was first assigned to all the levels in the primary school, I had to learn to smile, to laugh, to act, and even to scream. I am thankful that God directed me to teaching; otherwise, I would have taken life too seriously.

For me, teaching English is a mixture of challenges—often chaotic, sometimes dramatic, but also humorous.

In my early years of teaching, I noticed that pupils who were good in English were not so good in Math. Conversely, those who were good in Math were not so good in English. I also observed that primary school children were more interested in reading an English piece that was first explained to them in their language. The use of two languages in introducing new words or unlocking difficulties seemed to be more desirable among school children than giving meanings of new words in English.

For example, when the word "creature" was introduced to the students, I explained it as, "*Uray ania a naiparsua.*" If I had said, "This is anything that is created or made," only a handful would understand the meaning of the word.

One other time, I told the children to use the word *raise* in a sentence. The following sentences were volunteered:

"Raise your hands if they are clean," the class sang.

"The new raise car is lost," declared Rudy.

"I will e-raise the blackboard," said Ralph.

I then decided to give them the word in Ilokano. The children's faces suddenly lit up. Soon, Henry said, "I raise chickens in the backyard."

"The farmers raise pigs in the farm," stated Micca.

"The two boy scouts raised the flag for the singing of the Philippine national anthem," declared Camille.

It was a joy to listen to the students offer new and correct sentences.

I was a neophyte teacher when I was asked to be a substitute in the first grade. In my first class, I spoke in clear but simple English. No one responded to my questions. I then said, "*Ubbing, sinsinan uken kayo, a. No agsardengak AW-AW kunayo. Naawatanyo?*" (Children, let's pretend you are puppies. If I stop, you reply AW-AW. Do you understand?)

"Aw-aw!" the children replied in unison.

I began to sing. "How much is that doggie in the window?"

"Aw-aw!" they answered.

"I do hope that doggie is for sale."

"Aw-aw!"

At last the class was listening, I thought. "*Huston a ngaruden ta agleksiyon tayon.*" (Enough with this so we can begin our lesson.)

"Aw-aw!" Laughter followed!

I then began to tell them a story in Ilokano, after which they exclaimed "Ma'am *nagpintas! Agistorya kanto manen ton bigat, a.*" (Ma'am how nice! Tell us another story tomorrow please.) I realized at that moment that I had become a good storyteller. I had begun to change from being shy and silent into a more animated and livelier me. I had learned to meet the unique needs of the children under my care.

Once, in my 3rd grade class, while distributing the English books, I asked my students, "Now how do you take care of your book?" "Don't cut the pages of the book," said Joel.

"*Ikkam balay dagiti libro.*" (Cover the book.) answered Letty. "Who can say that in English?" I challenged the students.

Everyone became quiet. Then Roland, a naughty boy who sat in the third row, exclaimed, "Give house the books!" I tried to hold my laughter. What a translation! Where on earth did he get that sentence?

In one lesson about the different uses of *live in, live on, and live at*, I asked my students, "Where do you live?" "I live in Laoag City," replied Dina, a girl with a boyish haircut.

"I live on a farm," said Lolita, a short and chubby girl.

"I live at 27 General Luna Street," reported Isabel, the neatest student in the class.

"And what about you, Carlo?" I directed my question to Carlo who wasn't paying attention as he was having an argument with Henry, the boy beside him. Surprised at my question, Carlo retorted, "I will bring leaves tomorrow,

Ma'am." Laughter! Poor boy, I thought. He confused his English class for Science.

At another class where the lesson was on verbs, I noticed that a girl was sobbing at the back of the class. "What's wrong, Divina? Tell me," I asked. "Ma'am because Dimple and Sheen Gay are whispering to each other while looking at me. They are writing something on the paper. They are drawing ugly faces of me," Divina said between sobs.

I was annoyed because I was interrupted while writing verbs on the blackboard. In my frustration, I angrily demanded to see the sheet of paper Dimple and Sheen Gay were writing on. I was expecting to get angry at the two naughty girls. To my surprise, what I saw were not drawings but a list of names. The two had been writing names of classmates they were to invite for a birthday party. The list included Divina's name.

The students were all looking at me. I felt embarrassed at my decision to rush to conclusions about the two girls. And then I blurted, "Okay class, who can give me action words to describe what just happened to your classmates?" I managed to salvage the situation by directing the incident back to the lesson about verbs.

As a teacher, English is always uppermost in my mind. I realized this only after one incident at the end of the school year. The pupils were preparing to return their books. There was so much noise and commotion while I was collecting the books. In the chaos, I lost my cool and started to scream. But instead of ordering the students to quiet down, I found myself screaming, "Growing in English!" It was the title of the book I was collecting. As expected, the students did not quiet down and only made more noise.

I smiled to myself. At that moment, I thought growing in English was what I had been experiencing. Thanks to teaching English, I have learned to relish every moment and experience—whether they are quiet or chaotic moments or experiences with disciplined or unruly students. Every moment with my students transforms me.

The Tough Get Going

MARILYN C. BRAGANZA
Baguio National School of Arts and Trades, Davao City

My story may not be the greatest story ever told, but I always take pride in telling it over and over again. I may not be the best storyteller, but my students are. It is their stories that I share here.

I was a teacher from a private school when I decided to try my luck in the public sector. I knew exactly what to expect. My new setting, a public school, called for hard work and dedicated labor. I convinced myself that this might be where real teaching began. True enough, my expectations were met.

I was assigned to a school where students had a mix of tongues. Some spoke with a heavy Bagobo accent, while others spoke in the more dominant languages of the South. Those with heavy Bagobo accents usually lacked the confidence to perform in my classes. One such student was Jolan, a boy in my Bridging Class who refused to participate during oral drills. Because his written output was really not bad, I often wondered why he would not speak in my class. In my frustration, I found myself threatening to move him to another class. He then confessed that he spoke to only three students in school who happened to be his relatives; he was afraid of being ridiculed by his classmates.

At that moment, I realized that I only had two options available to me: fail him or teach him. I decided on the second option. Every week I spent one hour with Jolan to build his self-confidence and make him realize that it was okay to be different. It was not easy talking to a 13-year old boy who saw me as an English-speaking monster.

Other than my students' low self-confidence, I also had to grapple with their short attention span. How could I forget that day when the school's English Coordinator visited my class for a quarterly observation! That day, my focus skill was listening and I read aloud Emily Dickinson's "The Frigate." I was delighted to observe the students listening intently to my reading, or at least they pretended to listen, as I uttered each word with the appropriate gesture and facial expression. After the read-aloud session, I asked a series of comprehension questions to which not a single reply was correct. It was a disaster!

I am almost sure that what happened in my class that day is a typical occurrence at any public school. But that didn't mean that I would simply shrug it off and let the matter go.

The day after that disastrous class observation, I gave out copies of the text I had read aloud. Because the students knew that I had spent my own money to reproduce the text, they sensed my declaration of war on ignorance. They forced themselves to read! What followed was an enjoyable exchange of ideas. I then realized that listening was not a substitute to reading, and that these two skills, although related, were separate fields that must be approached differently.

In my school, we are expected to make full use of technology to teach the students. Just imagine how wonderful it would be if my students could search the Web about anything from the plays of Shakespeare to the Harry Potter novels of JK Rowling! There are, however, only ten computer units allotted to more than eight hundred students in my school. For these students, the idea of computer technology is abstract and non-existent. Honestly, these magical gadgets tell me one thing—I can still teach without them. I have always believed that when the going gets tough, the tough get going.

I have also come to realize that the English language is more accessible to the rich. Take the case of Nerissa. This 15-year old girl walks two and half kilometers to and from school every day. How can I expect her to be as attentive as those who are not as tired and sweaty when they get to the classroom? Nerissa belongs to a typical poor family of seven children and a father who worked as a laborer at a local banana plantation. If Nerissa had ten pesos a day, she could take a ride instead of walk to school. If she had ten pesos a day, she might have been more interested in the listening tasks. If Nerissa's family had electricity at home, she could have written better reports. If her home had electricity, she would have turned in better homework assignments.

There are many Nerissas in my classes. And their situation is a given. I have no means of making big changes in their lives. But I can try to understand their weaknesses. Once, a student complained that he hated my class because I always spoke English. Still, I don't code-switch to the vernacular. I try very hard to make the students produce the long /a/ sound, though I understand why some have great difficulty. I try to understand their situation when they jumble words while reciting a literary piece. I understand them when I catch them sleeping in class. But understanding does not mean giving up and letting go. On the contrary, I insist on making the students go through lots of tongue twisting exercises. And of course, I always try my best to keep their attention.

What I have learned from all these is that there is a specific solution to every sort of learning problem.

If there is one lesson I can share with English teachers who aspire to survive in the public school system, it would be this—Teach students what is ideal, but never deprive them of what is essential. Like many English teachers, I accept that I am a perfectionist who is often strict in observing rules. Wrong spelling is wrong! Subject and verb disagreement? Also wrong! But judging written work is not the same as judging young people. In teaching a language, successful communication is still the ultimate goal. When once a naughty boy who tried to impress his English teacher exclaimed, "I was absent Ma'am because my stomach was ouch," I congratulated him for communicating his message successfully. Letting him feel that he was understood was the best motivation for learning.

Teaching English in a public school is indeed sacrifice and joy rolled into one. The task is definitely difficult, but I am having fun. And my students are my greatest rewards. As long as I see smiles on their young faces, frowns that betray doubt but reflect question; as long as there is a Nerissa running to my classroom, catching her breath, and trying to listen to my read-aloud sessions; as long as I see desire in my students' eyes, I will go on and on and on.

To Do the Best until the End

DESIREE CALVERO HIDALGO
Urdaneta City National High School, Pangasinan

I was a young, fresh graduate when I received my first teaching assignment at the National High School of my town. Full of confidence and enthusiasm, I believed that I could tackle all the challenges teaching had to offer me. After all, the high marks I received in all my English courses in college should tide me over in teaching the language. Why worry then?

As I was a neophyte teacher, I was assigned to handle the sections of third year high school with the slowest learners. I must hasten to add that at this time, in public high schools during the 1980s, the underachievers, the bullies, the troublemakers, and other so-called rejects were lumped together in the lower sections. I was, of course, amply warned about the difficulty of instilling discipline among these "problem" students.

And so one rainy day in June, I found myself face to face with my first set of students. When I entered the room, all the talking and shouting ceased immediately. "The quiet before the storm," I thought to myself. With an uneasy smile, I greeted the class, "Good morning." The students returned the greeting with emphasis on "Madam."

I introduced myself as the English teacher. After I wrote my full name on the blackboard, the gates of hell suddenly flew open as giggles turned to guffaws and heehaws. The students laughed at my maiden name, Calvero, which one of the big boys pronounced as "Caldero." I was flabbergasted and wanted to flee. It seemed like an eternity before I could even utter a word. In my anger, I wanted to spew venom and get back at the students for their insolence.

But those little sparks of fury would not burn. I decided to ignore the students' disrespect and exclaimed, "Okay class. I admit that the Calvero clan to which I belong is closely related to the Calderos, the Calderetas, and others in the Ilocos region."

"What's in a name?" I added. "A rose by any other name would smell just as sweet." No one dared to call me Ms. Caldero again. This first encounter with my students ended in a friendly atmosphere as each student introduced himself or herself to me. Each student then stated what each wanted to become in the future.

In my classes, errors in grammar and pronunciation were pointed out on the spot. When a student, for instance, wanted to be excused so he or she may "pass water" or "irinate," I would immediately provide the correct expressions and even offer more creative ones:

"Excuse me, madam. Personal necessity calls."

"May I be excused madam? I need to pay a visit to the C.R."

Daily drills in my classes included drawing the students' attention to grammatical errors and mispronunciations. The students loved correcting themselves and using new and colorful expressions. Even excuse letters became sources of lessons and laughter.

> *Dear Madam:*
> *Please excuse me for my absent yesterday because my mother is born again.*

It had taken some time before I realized that my student's mother had given birth to another child.

Another letter read:

> *Dear Madam:*
> *I am absent tomorrow because I will help my mother die the chickens for my father's birthday. The goat will also die my father.*

In one lesson about gender, I asked the students what the English term was for female pig or male pig. *Takal. Takong.* A roar of laughter ensued as the students offered the Ilocano terms instead. One student mentioned that her father was nicknamed *Takal* or boar. Such nickname was customary in the barrios to refer to womanizing men with many children. *Takong* was the nickname appended to the female counterparts. The students then shared other monikers. *Dueg*, the Pangasinan term for carabao, is associated with one who is dark-skinned, muscular, and strong. To be called *Pusa* means that one is perceived to be small, quick-moving, and agile.

I seized that moment to intensify the students' attention to zoomorphism[1] by introducing English words that point to animal-like characteristics: feline,

---

1 This term refers to the tendency of viewing human behavior in terms of animal characteristics.

like a cat; canine, like a dog; bovine, like a cow; ovine, like a sheep; and porcine, like a pig. The students went home with a new set of words. I was amused to hear one boy who said to one girl, "Your voice is so lovingly feline," to which the girl promptly replied, "And you have a canine smile." The students were learning new words by actually using them in their own creative ways. And they were enjoying the humor each new word evoked.

We soon added more new words to our list:

- Simian – resembling a monkey
- Saurian – like a crocodile
- Caprine – like a goat
- Aquiline –like an eagle
- Ursine –like a bear
- Ophidian –like a snake

How the students enjoyed using the new words to describe their classmates! Soon, their sentences became more sophisticated, their expressions more creative: "ophidian embrace," "saurian smile," "simian looks," "porcine nose."

My first teaching assignment in a public school was characterized by many high points. But I also had my share of low points. One low point was the time I felt so dejected and so demoralized that I decided quit to the teaching profession altogether. I joined the Land Bank of the Philippines, which offered a higher pay and better working conditions. Still, I felt a deep longing and a strong desire to go back to teaching. There seemed to be an invisible string that connected me to my young wards. I missed the shared laughter, the wide-eyed innocence, even their impertinence and irreverence.

The experiences in my first teaching assignment were defining moments that determined the path I was to tread in my professional life. And as I grew older, my ardent desire to touch young lives grew stronger. My students from the lower sections may be ordinary kids who occupy the lower rungs of the intellectual ladder, but these same kids had given me rich insights and valuable lessons about life.

In their youthful midst, I learned patience, tolerance, resilience, hope. They made me laugh, but also cry. They brought me fresh views through their child-like innocence. They inspired me to become the best teacher I could be. Because of my students, I have dedicated myself to live by Abraham Lincoln's credo—"I do the very best I know how, the very best I can, and I mean to keep on doing so until the end."

The Red Carabao

DIONISIA B. FERNANDEZ
Salomague Norte Elementary School, Pangasinan

Over the years, reports about public education in the Philippines have pointed to an alarming decrease in English language proficiency among students, despite the use of English as a medium of instruction. The reports suggest deterioration in learning—a weak foundation in the public schools. I feel guilty knowing that public school teachers like me are partly to blame for this. Yet, I believe that it is also the public school teachers who can do something to make a change.

It may be impossible to transform most of the public elementary school children from carabao English speakers into proficient users of the language. Several factors come into play whenever we teach English: length of patience, range of interest, exposure to media. In addition, English is taught as a subject for a total of one hour a week in the elementary levels. And most public school children live in poverty. How then do we feed their heads if their families cannot feed their stomachs?

I believe public school children are intelligent children, if only they had more resources at their disposal. It is this perspective that pushes me to try everything possible to help my students learn and understand the English language.

One rule I have in my classroom is fairly simple: Speak only English! It was agreed that whoever broke this rule would pay a fine of one peso for each non-English word. For two days my students tried very hard to speak English only.

"Teacher, may I re-nate?" One pupil wanted to urinate. I used this opportunity to teach the students how to pronounce "urinate."

Later, I asked the students to check the work of their classmates. "Teacher, are we going to change papers now?" one pupil asked. I explained to them the difference between "change" and "exchange."

A week after imposing the Speak Only English campaign, I felt frustrated not because the students' carabao English worsened, or that the class treasurer did not collect a single peso, but because most of my pupils chose to keep their mouths shut. The campaign was a failure!

I decided to change my strategy. I decided to teach vocabulary, reading comprehension, and grammar in the simplest way possible. Within a week, the students were given a list of words for spelling practice. Five of these words were to be used in sentences. Pre-tests and post-tests were given every Monday and Tuesday, respectively. On Wednesdays and Thursdays, the students had paragraph dictation. During remedial sessions, the students were asked to read silently and then work independently on activity cards I had prepared.

The students were overwhelmed! As I had anticipated, the more activities they performed, the more they felt alienated by the English language. But I did not give up.

I tried another strategy. I asked the students to translate 20 Filipino words into English. From this activity I discovered how very limited my students' vocabulary were. *Permanship* (instead of penmanship), *residential table* (presidential table), *kindergarden* (kindergarten).

One day I asked the class to use the words "deduct" and "defense" in sentences. Juan, a rather naughty boy, boasted of the following:

"Deduct jump defense," Juan wrote. I tried to guess what the sentence meant. "Kindly translate your sentence into Filipino," I asked Juan.

"Why Teacher?" Juan scratched the back of his head. "Teacher, can you not…er…understood the sentence?"

"Understand!" I corrected Juan while controlling my laughter.

"Same same madam. You are ma-art," he said, smiling. I laughed.

"*Lumipad ang bebe sa bakod,*" Juan exclaimed.

"You mean, the duck jumped over the fence." I wrote the correct sentence on the blackboard.

Because of poor vocabulary, students like Juan often have difficulty expressing their ideas. Formal theme writing had become a burden to them. One time, I asked the students to write a diary entry about their Christmas vacation. Juan wrote:

Last Christmas, me and my family go in Ilocos and visit our families. I meat new frend. Name is David. We eat their house. We change gifts. I am very happy.

Knowing Juan's ability, I almost jumped for joy after I read the diary entry. Despite the grammar weaknesses, the message of the entry was clear. I felt a sense of achievement.

Another strategy I practiced to increase my students' vocabulary is DEAR, or Drop Everything And Read. This reading program encouraged students to bring their own storybooks to read in school. I also went to a book sale and purchased more storybooks for our mini-library. I was delighted at the students' enthusiasm for reading stories.

Of course, reading alone was not enough. It was imperative that the children understood what they read. I introduced a reading workshop that was held twice each month. In this workshop, pupils choose a storybook to read and the teacher would go around to ask about the stories. After some time of independent reading, the children would take turns talking about the stories they read.

Our first reading workshop was a disaster; only two pupils managed to recall what they had read. The rest only named the titles and authors of the books. At the last reading workshop, however, there was a noticeable improvement. Some students were actually eager to share their stories to the class.

"The story I read was *The Jungle Book 2*," Venice volunteered. She was the brightest student in my class. "In this story," she continued, "Baloo the bear got Mowgli from the village. Mowgli's friends Shanti and Ranjan followed. The bad tiger wanted to eat Mowgli. Before the tiger could eat Mowgli, he was saved by Shanti and Baloo. They were happy at the end of the story."

Myrell, another student, shared a story entitled *The Dumpy Wizard's Party*. It was about an old fellow who loved to give parties. After Myrell had shared her story, naughty Juan stood up.

"I have a question for Myrell," Juan said.

"What question would you like to raise?" I replied.

"Ahh…" Juan scratched the back of his head, a mannerism that had become his trademark. "Myrell what is the lesson of the story?"

I was speechless for a moment, realizing that Juan's question was the usual question I ask. Myrell bit her lower lip, thought for a few seconds, and then replied, "Don't trick other people."

I then asked Juan the same question he asked Myrell. Juan smiled and said, "Don't trust a policeman." We all laughed. Juan later shared his story with all of us.

Juan's simple ways amazed me. Once I asked the pupils to draw their favorite animal and write something about it. Juan drew a carabao and colored it flaming red.

"Have you not seen a carabao before, Juan?" I was irritable that day because I didn't sleep weil the night before. "Change your drawing," I demanded.

Juan quietly returned to his seat. Later, when I marked the students' works, I discovered that Juan did not change his drawing. Below the red carabao, Juan wrote:

This is my favorite animal. It is big. It works hard. Now it is colored red because it is mad. Father wanted to sell it to buy tractor instead.

Juan's words broke my heart. No matter how naughty he was, Juan had actually inspired me to design creative ways of making English meaningful to my students.

Hello, Miss Slow Down

SHIRLEY JEAN V. SUGANO
Macopa Elementary School, Compostela Valley

A bubbly talker but quite a reader—that was how my first grade teacher, Mrs. Melerita Anuta, described me when I was six years old. This teacher taught her students using such beautifully made materials that inspired us to read; we loved to read the names of every store, bakery, and pharmacy. She awakened my curiosity about all the words around me.

One weekend, my parents, siblings, and I traveled to the city to visit my aunt and uncle. I was always excited during such travels. The trip was delayed because of heavy traffic; the roads were undergoing repair. I noticed a sign that said "Slow down." At my relatives' house, there was another sign that said "Slow down." When I got out of the car, I told my father, "Slow Down must be a rich man. He owns every road from the town up to here in Aunt's house." Everyone burst into laughter. "One thing was sure," my Tatay Eddie announced. "She can read!" And as he hugged me, he whispered to my ear, "Hello, Miss Slow Down."

For sixteen years as a public elementary school teacher, I've shared such memories of the past with my pupils to encourage them to learn English.

When I was a neophyte teacher in a remote area of Casoon Elementary School, Monkayo District, I played Mother Dalmatian to my 101 grade one pupils. Their noise was tolerable, but I could not stand their smells, especially in the afternoons. Soon, I began to address them by their smells rather than their names.

After some time, I noticed that some students had not been coming to class. "Where are your classmates?" I asked the pupils who were present. I was shocked by the replies.

"Well, Mother Dalmatian can't stand their smell."

"Mother Dalmatian should give a bath to her 101 Dalmatians for them to smell good."

"Teacher Dalmatian does not love them anymore."

"We are just dogs anyway."

I didn't realize that I had hurt their feelings. I didn't realize that my pupils looked up to their teachers as their models who were sometimes considered even more reliable and correct than their own parents. I realized that I had failed to provide quality teaching to my 101 pupils.

In my classes, I encourage my students' parents to participate in their children's learning. I ask the parents to affix their signatures in their children's notebooks after the children had done their assignments at home. One girl who was a good reader did not have a single signature in her notebook. When I asked her about this, she cried. "Papa and Mama can't read and write, Ma'am. Neither can Kuya and Ate." After that incident, I reminded myself to be more sensitive to my students' feelings.

Teaching reading in the public schools is truly a difficult task. English teachers are often faced with pupils who were promoted to the next level even if they had not yet fully developed their reading skills.

Fred, a first grade student, used to play and talk to his classmates a lot, especially during recess time. But what I loved about him was that he was a good listener who was always quiet during reading lessons. Every day, I read aloud a story or a poem to my class. I read each line slowly and asked the class to repeat after me. After every line, I asked questions. Friday was usually individual reading time. Once, Fred approached me with confidence on his face. With a big book in his hand, he recited the famous poem "All Things Bright and Beautiful." I was overwhelmed with the speed of his reading. But as I slowly leaned towards the big book he was holding, I discovered that Fred was not actually reading. He had memorized the lines of the poem. His classmates applauded, but I just smiled and tapped his shoulder and said, "I'll ask you to read another poem tomorrow, Fred." He blushed and then confessed that he could not read.

There are so many students like Fred in classrooms throughout the country. But these students are not properly identified or even assessed. Having taught reading for many years, I discovered that storytelling truly helps in teaching reading and ensuring comprehension. Children love beautiful and colorful books. But in situations where there are no books, the teacher's illustrations are just as useful in teaching reading. One time, my students had an argument while I was having a storytelling session with them. "No, it's a carabao. Ma'am Shirley said so," I overheard a student say. But the other student objected, "No, it's a cow. It is wearing a loose-fitting dress."

I looked at the pictures they were arguing about. Right then, I apologized at the kind of drawings I had for the storytelling session. Oh, how I envied those teachers who had the artistic skill to illustrate any story!

Teachers are not perfect. It is important that teachers be open to criticism, even from their own pupils. We point out our pupils' mistakes; our pupils can also draw our attention to our own mistakes. Teachers should really be more mindful of their actions as there are so many sets of eyes observing what teachers say and do.

Sometimes, I mispronounce words. This happened rather frequently after I was transferred to the sixth grade. Having come from the first grade, I found myself adjusting to a totally different environment. In the first grade, I code-switched from English to the vernacular. But we were discouraged from doing this in the higher grade levels.

I often reminded my students to be aware of the differences between writing text messages and writing sentences in English. One day, while writing on the blackboard with a cell phone in one hand and a piece of chalk in the other, I wrote the text message instead of the lesson on the blackboard. When I realized what I had done, I felt totally embarrassed and immediately apologized. I promised myself that I would keep my cell phone in my bag during class periods.

I have never believed in fast-tracking the teaching of language to pupils. Fast-tracking does not produce good results. As in farming, one reaps a good harvest only after carefully sowing seeds, applying the right fertilizer with the right techniques, watering the plants daily, and taking proper care of these plants until full growth. To teach patiently one day at a time—that is what I can offer my students. Such endeavors do not require speed.

I was once designated as Master Teacher in the division of Compostela Valley. As I was the youngest Master Teacher at that time, I felt truly challenged. I had become responsible not only to students, but to other teachers as well. The professional development of teachers is oftentimes neglected. And school administrators continue to remind us to update ourselves on the latest trends of education. But teaching pupils every day is still the primary task of all teachers.

Elementary school children are notoriously unpredictable so teachers must expect the unexpected. Teachers must be flexible and aware. Teachers must approach the students' needs with 100% commitment to service, plus 101% trust in the Lord. With this formula, I am quite sure of 201% success of any endeavor.

I have traveled far in this teaching journey. The journey may be a slow one, but it is also a meaningful one. I am very sure that my Tatay is very proud of me. Tatay may not have been around to witness the teaching awards I received, but I can still feel his hug and still hear his whisper, "Hello, Miss Slow Down."

An English Teacher Wears Many Hats

MARISSA L. ARAMBULO
Santa Rosa Elementary School Central I, Laguna

Teaching English as a second language in Philippine public schools is a very challenging task for a teacher like me. However, many interesting, hilarious, and often heartwarming experiences enrich the four walls of my classroom.

I come from a family of teachers, being the daughter of a retired high school teacher. My aunt, who also taught for so many years, even became an old maid because of her dedication to the teaching profession. I have many cousins who are also mentors like me. I can say that teaching was, and still is, our lifeblood.

My first teaching stint was as a substitute teacher to a grade six adviser who was on maternity leave. For two months, I became so engrossed in my teaching assignment. I literally brought home all the books I needed for my lesson plans. It wasn't easy. But in my heart, mind, and soul, teaching is what I wanted to do for the rest of my life.

After my two-month stint as a sixth grade substitute teacher, I was assigned to the first grade. Many say that one must really be smart, patient, innovative, and creative in order to handle the grade one pupils. I was only twenty-three years old when I taught grade one. I was assigned to the section with the slowest learners. Sometimes, I thought to myself, "Poor me." But that didn't hinder me from continuing with this noble profession. The pupils had become my inspiration and they taught me the value of perseverance. So instead of sulking, I helped my poor-performing pupils learn to read and write.

The greatest test of my ability as a teacher happened during this period when I taught first grade. My pupils looked forward to the colorful and beautiful pictures that I cut out from magazines and used in my lessons. It was truly a challenge to face those seven-year old kids with their minds seemingly *tabula rasa*, as they looked forward to each new lesson every day. One mother told me that her son was so interested in the things I had taught him that the boy seemed to be more interested in what I had to say than in what his mother had to say.

Teaching English to Grade one pupils required skills in drawing. I wasn't too keen on art, but I tried my best. In first grade classrooms, it is expected for the blackboard to have drawings or cutout pictures pasted on it. One time, I even put labels on all the objects inside the classroom. I did this so that my pupils would know the names of things around them. The children formed the habit of reading the labels and became familiar with the names of these objects.

One quiet day, while preparing lessons after classes, a pupil approached me and asked if he could stay and read the words written on the blackboard. I was delighted at the thought that someone was truly enjoying the things we were doing in class. I allowed him to stay in the room and even helped him read some words.

This is only one of the many experiences I can never erase from my mind. In my early years of teaching, I was a substitute teacher, an artist, a mother's competitor, all rolled into one—the English teacher. All these experiences taught me to cherish the difficult days as a neophyte teacher. One such day was when I taught English to sixth grade pupils in one of the barrios in Sta. Rosa, which was still a town at that time. We were having a lesson about silent letters in some English words of French origin.

"Okay class, let us try to read these unfamiliar words," I announced.

"Here are those words, can you read them correctly?"

The students then recited.

bouquet   chalet   buffet   ballet   chateau   plateau

The students read the words with the "t" pronounced. I wasn't at all surprised because I made the same mistakes when I was learning to read. As a student, I tried very hard to overcome the mispronunciations. And now that I had become a mentor, I only laugh at that experience.

In our school, the "English-speaking Policy" was introduced at the opening of classes. It was not easy at first, but as months passed, the pupils got used to the practice of speaking only English. Under this policy, the pupils were only allowed to speak in the vernacular during the Filipino and HEKASI subjects, as well as during the EPP periods. I always reminded them to practice even during recess and at home. One time, my student Jerico told me in Tagalog that he wanted to urinate. I advised him to say, "Ma'am, may I leave the classroom?" With just that simple question, I would surely give him permission, I explained. After that day, all my pupils used the same line whenever they had to attend to their personal needs.

As an English teacher, I always see to it that at the end of each day, my pupils learn something from me. Whenever I ask them to write a two-paragraph theme, they often inquire about a certain Tagalog word that they would like to be translated into English. One pupil asked me what "*ipinagmamalaki*" was in English. She asked if her sentence was correct.

"I'm bragging about my family," she said. I grinned and then told her to make another sentence without using the word "bragging" because this had a negative connotation.

After a few minutes, she came to me and happily showed me another sentence.

I am proud of my family.

"That's better," I said. She was ecstatic and thanked me profusely. At that point, I decided to become more careful about giving translations to my pupils, as I wanted to encourage them to use a thesaurus or a dictionary whenever they needed to look up a word.

Not only was I my students' walking dictionary, I was also the adviser of our English-language school paper *The Arch.* I was the paper's adviser for ten years and in those then years I had the task of coaching the student-writers. I am proud of *The Arch* because of its many accomplishments. My student-writers have competed and won in writing competitions such as the National Schools Press Conferences. Meg Anne was awarded the second place in Editorial Writing (English) in the 2004 National Schools Press Conference. Another pupil, Maringal, bagged the first place in Feature Writing (English) at the Regional Schools Press Conference. This enabled Maringal to join the 2005 National Schools Press Conference.

A teacher wears many hats, so to speak. She is not only a mentor of young minds, but also a mother, friend, companion, critic, coach, adviser, guidance counselor to her pupils.

I still vividly remember that day when I was still an intern at the Philippine Normal College Laboratory School in Manila. I asked my suitor, Omar, who later became my husband, to get me a big frog. "Why do you need it?" Omar wondered if I had delved into biology. I said I needed a big frog for my English lesson. When I arrived home from Manila, there he was, waiting with a big smile and a big frog inside a bottle. I was so grateful.

Omar passed away three years ago and I miss him dearly. But when I wear my many hats as an English teacher, I see him again in my mind, always ever supportive of my endeavors.

Excuse me Ma'am, what's the English word for...

MARIAM B. RIVAMONTE
Santa Cruz Central School, Marinduque

I have been an English teacher in the intermediate levels of a public elementary school for almost ten years. I must admit that teaching English is not an easy task. But one survives if one practices reflective teaching.

When I first met my advisory class one day in June, I asked my students to prepare a simple opening program. A student led the class and said, "Good morning, Ma'am. Good morning, classmates. Today, we are going to start our program!"

Then he continued, "The first number of our program is an opening prayer to be led by Charry." And so, the said pupil stood up and led the prayer.

Then the leader again stood up and introduced the next number. "The next number of our program is an opening song to the class," he declared. I just sat at the back of the class and observed the students go about their opening program. "And the last number of our program is a closing song to the class," the leader continued.

After the program, I went to the front of the classroom and said," Well, I appreciate what you presented this morning. You observed the correct order in conducting a program. But I think there is something lacking in your program. It has become predictable. You need to put or add some spice. You are no longer primary grade pupils. Why not try something creative, like an ASAP-style program?"

I then pointed out some weaknesses in their English, "Also, we say 'opening song *by* the class,' not '*to*' the class." With that statement, I had begun my lesson.

Teaching students the proper and systematic way of doing things would surely create an orderly classroom environment. However, English teachers must also be aware of the benefits of correcting mistakes at once so that their students would learn genuine communication. In addition, frequent repetition would help students practice their English speaking skills more.

In one lesson about speaking correctly, I asked the students to read aloud all the words in a spelling list and to create sentences using the words. One pupil raised her hand. "Ma'am, may I?" she volunteered. ""Yes, Camille," I said.

"The Philippines is a beautiful country," Camille uttered. "That is correct!" I replied.

"What about you, Pete?" Pete was a very shy pupil. When I called him, he smiled and looked at his classmates. He slowly stood up. Then he said, "The telephone is ring loudly." Some pupils immediately laughed, but I reminded these students to refrain from laughing at their classmates' mistakes.

"Oh, so, that is your sentence. But there's something wrong with your sentence, Pete," I said gently. Then I wrote the sentence on the board. I asked everybody to carefully study the sentence. "What do you think is wrong with this sentence, class?" I asked.

Then one pupil volunteered an answer. "Ma'am, the sentence should be *The telephone is ringing loudly.*"

"Very good!" I declared. Then I asked Pete to recite his sentence a second time. This he did with more confidence.

I then asked the class for more sentences using words from the spelling list. One student said, "I has many photos in my album." Again, I wrote the sentence on the board and asked everybody to read it. Then I asked the pupil who gave the sentence to read it aloud.

"Okay, but do you know that if your subject begins with *I* or *You*, your verb should always be in the plural form?" I asked him. "So is your sentence correct?"

"Ah..eh.. Ma'am.. *have,*" he beamed. With a smile, he declared, "I have many photos in my album."

Teaching correct grammar among students should always be done whenever the need arises. It should not be done only during the lesson proper. It is important for the students to always be aware and constantly be reminded about the rules of forming sentences, from simple to compound to complex sentences. If a student makes a mistake, it would not be beneficial to reprimand him or her because mistakes are normal among elementary school students. Reprimanding is not the way to correct or prevent errors as this only creates fear among the pupils and thus slows down their progress.

In one class activity, a pupil asked, "Excuse me, Ma'am. May I know the English word for *sawayin?*" I immediatey replied, "Refrain. Why do you ask?"

"Ma'am it's because Michael speak in Tagalog!" the pupil said. "Ma'am, she say that *pakisawayin mo nga yong kabilang grupo, maingay kasi.*"

"So, if you were the one to say that line in English, how would you say it?" I asked her. She kept silent for some time and smiled at me. Then she answered while scratching her head, "Eh Ma'am, should I say..aaa please aaa.. refrain aaa.... the other group for making noise? Am I correct Ma'am?" I was pleased by her effort to translate the sentences. I then nodded and told her to go on with her work.

One time, while I was delivering my lesson about adjectives and descriptive words, I asked the students to give me examples. One pupil raised his hand and then stammered with his question, "Excuse me Ma'am, eh.. eh.. I am an example. Ma'am, may I know the English word for *masipag?*" His classmates then protested his speaking in Tagalog. I simply ignored them and said, "*Masipag* is industrious in English."

I then asked the class to give the English words for Tagalog adjectives. Almost everybody raised their hands to answer. "*Malawak…mabango…madaldal… masikap…magalang…matipid…maramot...*" We had a wonderful time giving the English adjectives of those words, even if only a handful had the correct answers.

"Oh, you're all good students!" I declared at the end of the lesson. "You all tried to give examples of adjectives, which only means, you really understood our lesson. But I'm still a little bit sad that not all knew the correct answers." The students looked at me with their weary eyes and one pupil said, "Eh, Ma'am…. Eh…eh… sorry, we does not know them really."

At that moment, I could only be silent. Despite their carabao English, I felt that they were truly interested in learning the language. I then thought of other ways to help them become better speakers of English. I decided that every time they entered the classroom, I would greet each student in English and ask them to reply in English.

"Good morning!" I greeted each student.

"May we come in?" the students replied.

"Yes, you may," I answered.

"Oh, how's your day today?" I added

"Well Ma'am, I'm having a nice day today!" the students replied

With this simple daily greeting, the students express themselves in English in a simple and non-threatening way. With simple exercises, little by little and step-by-step, students learn to communicate well with others.

Teaching the students how to speak English could not be done in just the blink of an eye. The process to helping students learn to use the language correctly is a long and complex one. Practice makes perfect—if only English teachers remember this everyday. In addition, we should always remember that we couldn't teach our students how to speak English correctly unless we ourselves know how to speak and express ourselves correctly. We must be patient not only with our students, but also with ourselves.

Oftentimes, my students are very naughty. One time, we talked about the story of Juan Tamad. I asked them who the characters were, where the story happened, and what happened to the characters in the story. Some students gave the correct answers. But when I moved to why and how questions, everybody kept silent and just stared at me. I then started to call them one after another.

"Jun? Why did mother get angry at Juan?" I asked

He stood up and looked at me. No answer.

Then I called another one, "John Paul?" No response.

"Rosy? Ken? Ronaldo? Mark Paulo?" No one knew the answer

I modified my question and asked them again. "What did Juan Tamad do that made his mother angry?" Still nobody had the guts to answer until one pupil raised her hand, "Excuse me Ma'am,"she said. "Eh, ma'am, what's English for *ipinagbili niya sa palaka ang kanyang mga tindang rice cakes.*"

Then I replied, "He sold the rice cakes to the frogs."

I told her. " Ma'am *yon po*!" she declared. I smiled at her and then I asked her to stand up and recite the answer.

Then I continued, "Do you think it is right for the mother to get angry at Juan?" The class then had an interesting discussion about the story.

" Excuse me Ma'am," one pupil interrupted the discussion. "What's English for *dahil mali ang ginawa niya.*" I paused for a moment. That question again, I thought.

Whew! English is really difficult to teach among Filipino pupils. Often, I find myself translating Filipino phrases or sentences into English so the students can truly comprehend a story. In the Philippines, teachers of English really need to be patient. We need to burn our eyebrows and think of creative solutions to help our students become good speakers of English. Instant remedies do not work—only gradual, step-by-step strategies do.

The Rewards of Teaching English

My English Teaching Journey

MARIA VILLAMIN PINEDA
Marinduque National High School, Isok Boac, Marinduque

lese escuse me for being absent today because I am six.
This line is from one of the first excuse letters I found on my teacher's table some thirty-eight years ago. I was not prepared to read such a shocking piece on my first year of teaching. Since then, I have received countless other letters of excuse, but it is this one that challenged me to stay on as an English teacher for more than three decades in a public high school in my home province of Marinduque.

My journey as an English teacher is like the sea-travel I take from the port of Balanacan to the port of Dalahican in Lucena. Every school year, we launch our ships in June and arrive at the port of destination in March. Like the sea, each school year is filled with unpredictable events, from the very smooth to the very rough conditions that may wreck boats.

In this voyage, I have survived various curriculum revisions of the Department of Education—from the Two-Two Plan of the College Preparatory and Vocational Curriculum of the 1970s, to the Secondary Education Development Plan (SEDP) of the 1980s, and through the current Basic Education Curriculum (BEC) innovations.

In 2003, in its desire to upgrade the level of communication proficiency of secondary teachers, the Department of Education administered a Self-Assessment Test to all teachers of English, Science and Mathematics. I was happy to receive one of the top scores in the Division. I have since been assigned to the Mentoring Program. For me, this achievement, and my having been earlier promoted to Master Teacher I, are the significant turning points in my teaching career.

When I first applied for a teaching position in the 1970s, the Superintendent was very hesitant to accept me because I was as thin as a reed. He probably thought that I would not be able to hurdle the physical rigors of classroom teaching. Like him, I was apprehensive. I studied at an exclusive all-female private college; the only exposure I had to a public high school was the few months of practice teaching with a teacher-adviser always present to assist me.

I was nineteen years old when I first set foot on Marinduque National High School. On my first day, I already wanted to back out. My students were just a few years younger than I was. For the first few months I had to endure sneers and catcalls behind my back. During rainy months, the students teased me about being swept away by the wind. I tried all sorts of vitamin supplements to make me look bigger and heavier. One colleague suggested that I get married and immediately bear children, as this was a guarantee of gaining weight.

I took the advice seriously. As I didn't have a boyfriend, I decided to accept the overtures of a male co-teacher who also taught English like me. Together, we sang *You've Got a Friend* and *Bridge Over Troubled Waters* as motivation for new lessons in English. He later because my husband. But married life and motherhood did not increase my weight. Instead, my devotion to the teaching profession grew immensely.

The secret to becoming a seasoned English teacher is passion for reading. This is why I have permanently stationed my worktable inside the library to be near the newspapers and magazines that I voraciously read during short breaks. Though busy with my duties as a wife and a mother, notwithstanding the lesson plans that I had to prepare everyday, I take time to read. I scrimp when buying new clothes, bags, and shoes so I will have money to buy the latest bestsellers.

One book I remember reading in a record three hours was Sidney Sheldon's *The Other Side of Midnight.* I read this during the period of frequent power outages in the province. Once, while I was reading the most suspenseful part of the story, the lights went out. I immediately grabbed the flashlight and held on to it until I completed the last page of the book, much to the dismay of my husband who thought I was crazy.

What do I do after reading a book? I donate the book to the library. It delights me to watch others read and reread the books I donated. Apparently this practice of book donation had led to a chain of donations through the years as alumni bookworms and friends sent their used books and reading materials to the school library. Since then, book donation has become my advocacy and I hope to continue doing this as my legacy to the students of my school.

One article in a *National Geographic Magazine* which I read in the 1980s made me dream of traveling abroad. This article about the famous canals of Venice, Italy, truly fascinated me. I imagined myself in a Venetian gondola and kept this image of myself in my mind for many years. I wanted so badly to go Europe. As my salary as a classroom teacher was not even enough for my family's needs, I thought of other ways to save money so I could travel. I took on tutorial jobs after school. What I earned I saved in what I called my "dream bank." I set a definite timetable—I should realize my dream before I turned fifty.

I persuaded two childhood friends to dream with me. And finally, after twenty years of dreaming and saving, on my fiftieth birthday, I was able to fly halfway across the globe to the European countries that were only made familiar to me through the glossy pages of the National Geographic Magazines. My friends and I walked through the places where Jesus lived and died in the Holy Land. We prayed inside the magnificent churches of Rome and admired the breathtaking sight of Michelangelo's *Last Judgment* at the Sistine Chapel. I visited former students in the exotic land of Vienna, Austria. And of course, I was teary-eyed when the gondoliers hummed "O Sole Mio" while we traveled along the magical Venetian canals. I literally had to pinch myself several times to make sure that I was not dreaming.

After that dream trip, I was rich with experiences to share in the classroom. I often remind my students that reading does not only bring people to imagined places, but also pushes readers to transform dreams into realities.

Recently, a campus journalist asked me where I saw myself ten years from now. I was dumbfounded. Ten years from now I wouldn't be in the classroom anymore, I thought. Suddenly, I felt sad. I could not imagine myself *not* being an English teacher. To whom shall I share the very exciting tales of Homer's *Iliad and Odyssey*? What about all those book reports that I love to check and the high school memoirs that I look forward to reading? I would surely miss those funny letters of excuse that I always read at the beginning of each class.

I'm now counting a few more years before my retirement. My exciting journey as a classroom teacher is about to end. A *balikbayan* friend once commented about how popular I had become in my province as everywhere we went, there was always a former student who greeted me. One student even recited a line from Robert Frost's "The Road Not Taken," one of my favorite poems.

To date, with an average of three hundred students a year, I have handled almost ten thousand young minds who are spread out all over the world from consular offices in Europe to cruise and cargo ships, from hospitals in Saudi Arabia to hotels in Asia. Whenever the boat gets crowded, I always get a seat. There is always someone who helps me carry my heavy bags to the tricycle or the jeepney. This privilege of a teacher is so priceless. It is a treasure that I will cherish in my heart long after I say goodbye to the classroom.

This year is a remarkable year for my family. My daughter, Liv Uvy Lane, was recently promoted to manager in the bank where she works. She is married to a medical doctor and has given me my very first grandchild. My son, Lloyd Ivan, who is an instructor at a university, has just completed his Master's degree. And my husband, Lito, the one who sang songs with me to introduce our English lessons, will soon retire from government service after many years as a DepEd Specialist in English. For someone who is a simple English teacher, I look back on these thirty-eight years and feel a deep sense of satisfaction at what had become of my life.

Perhaps after my retirement, I will be "promoted" to pre-school teaching. I think I will read stories to my grandchildren and delight them with Adarna tales and Mother Goose rhymes.

The Ways I Love Thee

RHEA CHRISTINA U. RABIN
San Pablo City Science High School, San Pablo, Laguna

"Free, pure and passionate love does not exist!" I bluntly announced to my idealistic junior high school students after paraphrasing Elizabeth Barrett Browning's famous sonnet. What followed was a barrage of questions and arguments about the existence of ideal love. It was hard to play the devil's advocate in this informal debate, primarily because it pained me to go against my students' convictions. Moreover, it was not easy to speak against what I myself believed in.

I wrapped up the lesson on "How Do I Love Thee" with a declaration that I believed in love that knows no boundaries and carries no conditions. I was tempted to say, "Just as I love you." But I just left the room, more deeply in love with them.

HOW DO I LOVE THEE? LET ME SPEAK THE WAYS

Verbally, I express and share love to my students. Through teaching English, I discovered several lines synonymous to *I love you*. Every day, I greet my students with a jovial "Good morning," a sympathetic "How are you?", an affectionate "I missed you in class yesterday," a gratifying "What remarkable work!" and a heartfelt "I'm sorry" as ways of expressing my love. Even the chocnuts, lollipops, and cupcakes that I gave out as incentives for class activities demonstrate love.

Over the years, my synonyms for love increased such that even criticisms and reprimands were added to the growing list. My student Geri Mae drew my attention to this when she gave me a card that read: "I love how you criticize my work; it's not hasty, nor shocking, nor offensive." Amazingly, even when I was grumpy about my students' irresponsible behavior, they didn't feel disheartened.

Of course, there are several occasions when I speak directly of my love for them. My classic love line is "Win or lose, I love you." This line proved therapeutic, as both my students and I became more proud of the love that grew between us during competitions, more than the honor we brought back or left behind.

Just how much love my students are getting and giving is illustrated in the following poem crafted by the class after I had some conflict with them.

A FIVE-LETTER WORD
by III-Medeleev

The first two years, it's so dull and dim
We can't see light in this place so grim
A very bright star to come, it's our dream
To light us on this gloomy stream.

In the midst of our journey, a hymn extant
The sound of queer and murmuring chant
We became curious and followed the sound
At the end of the road, this lady we found.

God has given this gift from above
A gift of compassion and never ending love
Now we feel our hearts are in sob
We hinder the door from turning the knob.

We still remember the cupcake days
Who's the winner, we say hooray!
Now the cupcake's spoiled. Gray!
And she's going away with the cupcake's tray.

She turned to love our dislike and hate
Now we don't know what will be our fate
We hate ourselves for having this trait
We don't want to lose her before it's late.

We made a mistake, yes it's true
Down on our knees, we're begging you
To give us a chance and wipe out the blue
To take out our hearts from serious woes.

Sorry…this five-letter word we do
To unlock the door and see the sunshine through
We don't expect forgiveness, but we wish you knew
That we are trying to change because we love you.

HOW DO I LOVE THEE? LET ME LISTEN TO THE WAYS

National Scientist Alfredo Lagmay once said: "True love is silent and also truly quiet." This statement struck me. In moments of silence, my heart enlarges and enables me to become more sympathetic and compassionate. This is why it has become my mantra as a teacher to talk less and listen more. This I-Listen-You-Talk (ILYT) technique has proven beneficial especially to those muted by the traditional teaching practice of making students copy notes, remain quiet in class, and pretend to listen to the teacher.

Since I started teaching English, first as a Gurong Pahinungod (a University of the Philippines volunteer) in Pawa National High School, Cuyo, Palawan, then later, as a public school teacher in San Pablo City National High School, I thought I had already heard all the incredible stories about teaching English—until the following incidents happened to me. In one class, I wrote on the blackboard: *The boy covered his face with his hand.* Then came the most shocking question—"Ma'am, what is hand?" Silently, I marveled at the student's courage to even ask that question.

Another incident that taught me to listen intently to my students was during a debate on euthanasia. One student stood up and exclaimed—in halting English—that he would rather die while trying to pump oxygen into a relative's body, than allow that person to go. His earnest desire to sustain the life of a loved one, despite its seeming impracticability, silenced me. The boy inspired me to listen more.

I was amazed at how many messages silent acts carried. As I talked less and listened more, the atmosphere in my classroom became lighter. My silence also made me a receptacle of my students' most intimate thoughts. I recall having life-is-beautiful conversations with suicidal students. There had also been many occasions when I played counselor to students who needed enlightenment.

HOW DO I LOVE THEE? LET ME READ THE WAYS

Books are my most prized possessions. I am fortunate that, as an English teacher, I can share my treasures with my beloved students. One of them is the 1962 *Book of Verse* that belonged to my mother. Its red tattered pages contained the classic works of the greatest poets from Barrett to Browning to Wordsworth.

For me, reading poetry has always been the most enjoyable part of teaching English. Through poetry, I find pleasure in making the students appreciate the rhythm and rhyme of literary pieces such as William Shakespeare's sonnets. At first, Shakespeare's poems turned the students off. But after I helped them grasp the poems' intricacies, the students began to express genuine appreciation of the literary pieces by attempting to imitate them.

> My English Three
> *by Jordan Ferdin Halili*
>
> **M** is for many, things I have learned
> **Y**es, that's true, for new knowledge I earned.
> **E** is for essays, which are hard to do,
> **N**o matter what, they are enjoyable too.
> **G** is for the group activities, where we interact
> **L**ots of fun while learning is a fact.
> **I** is for idioms, their meanings explored,
> **S**earching all of them without getting bored.
> **H** is for happiness, our lessons bring,
> **T**eaches us everyday of new things.
> **H** is for the heart, where this subject had a part,
> **R**emains until we're far apart.
> **E** is for English III, that we have loved,
> **E**ver will stay in our hearts!

Poems offer the most splendid metaphors for love. Poems such as "Passionate Shepherd to his Love," "I Wandered Lonely as a Cloud," and "When I Consider How My Light is Spent" are some examples. There are a handful of my students who embraced poetry. As an incentive, I allowed them to access my books on poetry. And oh, as in Lord Byron's own words, *how they walk in beauty, like the light.*

HOW DO I LOVE THEE? LET ME WRITE THE WAYS

I love the printed word. And what better way to be intimate with the printed word than to teach English! My students' journals or notebooks have become channels through which I nurture my love for my students. Although I am constrained by the prescribed competencies in teaching English, I am still able to express myself through my written replies and comments on their work.

Less subtle are the letters I write to each of my students. They contain personalized messages and expressions of my love. And oh, I also get so many I-love-you in return.

> I Love English III and my Teacher
> *by Rose Ann Cayetano*
>
> I love English III because of my teacher
> She taught III-Neptune to have self-confidence.
> I love English because I learned a lesson;
> I learned how to say sorry to a person.

> I love this subject because I am active.
> Now I know the difference between wish and hope
> And I also know how to make an outline
> That is because of English and my teacher.
>
> I feel good when I am in front of her.
> I hope that I will be a good teacher someday
> And for me this is an unforgettable subject,
> Because I love English III and my teacher.

AND I SHALL LOVE THEE MORE—EVEN AFTER ENGLISH

I believe that teachers are the most loved creatures. It is normal to receive thank you notes and letters while mentoring students. But it is a rare prize to receive a note from a student who had already left the school. One such note is from Mark Marcos, now a Developmental Communication student at the University of the Philippines, Los Baños:

> I'm thankful she'd been part of my life.
> Words I can say to God if he asks me what I can say about you.
> You taught me many things and I'm using them right now in college:
> From journalism to photography to radio broadcasting.
> It's an edge for me, knowing these during my high school days.
> Thank you because you taught me all these things.

And then there is this email from Dianne Marie who placed fourth in the Nursing Board Examination: *Oh, by the way, do you still remember me? I was your student in English 102. I was really touched by your letter. I treasure what you said about me more than any medal or certificate ever given to me. Thanks. Ever since I got hold of your letter, I've been wanting to e-mail you to extend that I appreciate your kindness for admitting me to your class no matter how late I sought your help. And for the kind words that you've said about me, thank you so much. I still have your letter. I put it in a box of memorabilia that I'll be using for my scrapbook. That's how important it is to me.*

After reading such lines from former students, I have become more certain about my love for my students in English. In this certainty, I experience what William Wordsworth once wrote: *My heart with pleasure fills, and dances with daffodils.*

Elmo and English Time

HIPOLITO M. BERANO
Cajidiocan National High School, Romblon

I never thought that I would become an English teacher. I came into the exciting world of teaching when I was a fresh graduate of B.S. Fisheries from Aklan National College of Fisheries at New Washington. At that time, I was on vacation in my hometown Romblon. While waiting for a call regarding a job opportunity in Cebu, my parents informed me of an available teaching position at Romblon National High School, my alma mater. The principal, who was my former teacher, told me to report for an interview.

Soon I found myself in front of my former mentors, answering a series of questions. Although I majored in Inland Fisheries, which many thought to be a vocational-technical course, Mrs. Mazo was impressed by the way I responded to her questions as I displayed a full command of English. After that 15-minute very cordial and pressure-free interview, she told me to report to work in June.

I was shocked. "What subject will I handle, Ma'am?" I asked. "You will teach English 1 and you will be the coordinator of our Theater Arts Club," she replied.

"Why not Practical Arts, Ma'am, since it's my specialization?" I protested.

"We are in dire need of an English teacher. Or do you prefer Math?" she retorted.

"No Ma'am. Math is my waterloo. I prefer English."

I left the school feeling very confused. "An English teacher?" I thought to myself. "A fishery graduate… will be teaching English?"

But that shocking experience did not end there. On my first day of teaching, Mrs. Mazo assigned me to handle the section with the slowest learners in the first year, and since I was a neophyte teacher, I was not yet expected to wear the prescribed teacher's uniform.

It was the early 1980s and I would wear a pair of Levi's jeans and a t-shirt even when attending meetings and some official school functions. So on my first day of teaching, I tucked my class record at the back pocket of my *maong* pants and reported to school. When I got to my classroom, there was a long and crooked line of students—girls in front, boys at the back. I asked one hefty and tall boy who stood at the end of the line, "Is this section Ilang-Ilang?" He stared at me and with a disrespectful and threatening tone retorted, "YES! This is the last section. You better stand in front of me and not behind me!" As the flag ceremony was about to begin, I did not say anything.

After the flag ceremony, the usual introduction of new and old teachers did not take place because the principal was away. And so we all headed to our assigned classrooms and I marched straight to the teacher's table. I stood in front of the class for a few seconds and observed my students' faces, especially Elmo's (I learned his name later), as I introduced myself as their teacher. That first meeting, which my students thought would be a smooth one, became a scolding session about respect for elders, teachers, and superiors.

When the bell rang, everybody rushed out of the room except one boy. Elmo meekly approached the teacher's table and apologized to me. "Sir, I'm sorry. I never thought that you were our adviser. I thought you were just a classmate because you look like us. I thought teachers wore *barong* and not t-shirt and rubber shoes." I came to my senses and realized that I deserved half the blame. I accepted Elmo's apology but required him to submit a letter with a promise to avoid such disrespectful and arrogant behavior .

Later, I found Elmo to be a very responsible student. He was our instant carpenter, plumber, repairman, etc. When conflicts between his classmates arose, Elmo acted as mediator. I also learned why he had developed such broad shoulders and big muscles and looked much older than his classmates. "You know, Sir, I work in the marble quarries during weekends. I carve big marble blocks to support my schooling and that of my younger sister in the third year. Sir, we are poor and my father is also a lowly marble worker in Barangay Guimpingan," he once confided in me.

Our strong bond of friendship developed even more when I composed a song for my new lesson in English. It was getting more and more difficult to handle my class, which was the section with the slowest learners in that year level. I realized that my students had difficulty remembering the different parts of speech, their meanings, and examples. So I decided to write a song for them to sing whenever we had lessons on nouns, pronouns, and the like.

I didn't have an innate talent for music so I asked my students who among them could play the guitar. "Sir, Elmo can play the guitar," everyone exclaimed.

And so every afternoon after class, Elmo went to my advisory room and we practiced singing the song. After five practice sessions, we perfected the lyrics and melody. Elmo then became our instant music teacher in English.

With this song, my students achieved a better grasp of my lessons about the different parts of speech. The song became such an instant hit in the school that even my co-teachers in the English Department used it as a motivation song before they started their lessons.

How Wonderful Is English Time

We know, we know it's English time
And we will learn so many things
From reading poems and writing themes
And memorizing rhymes.

We understand what a noun is
The name of things we see around
An action word is called a verb
Like *hop*, like *dance* and *sing*.

An adjective describes a noun
Noun substitutes are called pronouns
An adverb also modifies
A verb and an adjective.

A preposition shows relationship
A conjunction joins the words in phrase
Hurrah! Oh! Gosh! interjections too
They show strong emotion.

How wonderful is English time
We enjoy all the lessons taught
Like subject and the predicate
And different parts of speech.

Elmo completed his first year of high school with me. After that year, I lost track of Elmo and did not know if he had graduated from high school.

After some years, I was surprised by a visit from Elmo. I was naturally glad to see him again, being my old and *special* student, who I could not forget. With him was a girl who he introduced to me. "Sir, this is Margarita, the girl I will marry soon… we came here, Sir, to invite you… to be *ninong*…We're getting married next month. I hope you will not fail us, Sir."

I could not utter a word. For me it was a great honor to be *ninong* for the first time to a young couple and a former student, too. "Sure, sure Elmo. It's a great privilege for me to be your *ninong*. Expect me to be present on your wedding day," I excitedly replied. I have heard that the couple has since been blessed with two children.

Many years have passed and now I am a school administrator. But sometimes when I am alone, fond memories of my being an English teacher and that meaningful encounter with Elmo still brings me joy and contentment. Reflecting on those unforgettable experiences with my students in English reminds me of valuable life lessons. To this day, I laugh at the thought that a fishery major like me had inspired young students through songs and lessons in English.

Dining with Dyna

APOLONIA MARITES O. HERNANDEZ
Sto. Niño National High School, Batangas City

Teaching is the noblest of professions. My professor in college often used this quote. In my twelve years of teaching English, I have proved the quote to be right. Teaching requires skill, innovation, resourcefulness, and patience. Dedication to the service, sympathy and concern for the welfare of the students—these are also primary requirements of teaching.

In my twelve years of teaching English, I have had various experiences that were often ridiculous, sometimes boring, sometimes exciting, but always inspiring. Every year, I meet all sorts of students—from the noisy to the attention-seeking, from the irritating to the slow. There are students who are poor in pronouncing words in English. There are students who are slow in reading. Still, I give my full attention to students who need my help and patience more.

I remember my first year of teaching. It was in a private school. In one lesson, I asked my students to give examples of nouns. One student said, "Cat." I praised him and then asked another student to give another example of a noun. One student blurted out, "Another cat." As a natural reaction, the whole class laughed loudly. Instead of getting angry, I remained composed and proceeded with the lesson. Soon, my students realized that I was serious with my lessons. They later became careful in giving their own examples of nouns.

My good and bad experiences in dealing with students never distracted me from my performance as a teacher. In 1996, I finally had the courage to take on a teaching post in a public school—the San Agustin National High School in Isla Verde, Batangas City. The school was very far from my place of residence. Despite this, I grabbed the opportunity to teach the students there.

To get to the school, I had to ride a boat every week and reside in San Agustin from Monday to Friday. This meant that I could not be close to my sick mother most days of the week. In the school, I met different sorts of students, but they had one common desire—to learn English.

Once, I had a lesson on syntax. The students were given an exercise on arranging jumbled words and phrases into a meaningful whole. When it was time to give the answer, a student volunteered to write on the blackboard: *The seashore was standing along the man.* I was so shocked that I couldn't react. Some students laughed loudly. So again I composed myself and asked the class, "In this sentence, what is the subject or who is standing?"

"The seashore," the students answered in chorus.

"Do you think the seashore can stand along the man?" I asked them again.

"No, Ma'am," they replied in chorus.

"So what is the right sentence?" I asked.

My bright student replied, "The man is standing along the seashore."

"Very good!" I praised him.

Teaching is full of sacrifices, but it is also full of rewards. This was proven one afternoon while I was strolling in SM Batangas to shop for some things I needed for class the next day. Inside the bookstore, I accidentally dropped my bag and all my things fell to the floor. Suddenly, a lovely lady in a green suit approached me and helped me pick up my things. "Here are your things, Ma'am," she said, smiling.

"Oh thank you. You are so helpful," I praised her.

Then the lady in green asked, "Ma'am, don't you remember me?"

I did not recognize her. She then introduced herself as my former student in San Agustin. "Oh, you are Dyna," I finally remembered. "You look so beautiful and tall now. When you were a first year high school student, you were small and thin, but now you are sexy and attractive," I told her.

"Ma'am, let me invite you to an early dinner. We can talk and I can tell you what happened to me after high school and after you left our school," she said excitedly. I wanted to turn down her invitation, but I was also curious to hear her story. So even though I worried about the time, I joined Dyna for dinner.

At the restaurant, while Dyna was choosing food to order from the menu, my many years in San Agustin flashed through my mind. Dyna—the small, shy, simple girl who sat at the back of the classroom. Look at her now, I thought.

There was one time in our English class when I wrote some words on the blackboard for all to read. I called on Dyna to read the words out loud. She stood slowly and hesitantly. "Dyna, please read the words on the board," I asked her a second time. Reluctantly, Dyna confessed that she couldn't read the words. I then I told her to repeat the words after me. "Outdoors," I said. "O-u-u –t doors," she slowly said. "Crocodile," I said. "C-c-c-ro- co-dile," she replied. I realized at that moment that Dyna was one student in my class who could not read well. I decided to formulate a strategy to help these students.

Soon, I designed a reading program and presented this to my principal for approval. My principal was so delighted with the proposal. He gave his full support and even helped me in finding materials for my remedial reading class. The next day, I met Dyna at our school library and told her to come to school early every day and to bring a packed lunch. I explained to her that she would undergo remedial reading sessions. We had two thirty-minute sessions every day—one at seven in the morning and another at twelve-thirty in the afternoon. Her parents were also notified about this program.

Dyna was a diligent student. Every day she went to school early in the morning and met me in the library. She had lunch in the classroom and at for her afternoon session, she went back to the library for the continuation of our sessions. One hour daily we devoted to her remedial reading lessons. It was difficult at first to teach Dyna how to read, but she improved gradually. After two or three months, she learned to read fast. "Dyna, you are a better reader now. Do you practice reading at home?" I asked her. "Yes, ma'am. I read at home what you give me to read in school. And I read other books, too, ma'am," she told me.

Very good, I praised her. But I want to tell you that next week, I will move to Sto. Niño National High School because my husband wants me to teach in a school near our residence. I hope you won t stop reading and you will continue what I taught you and told you to do, I explained.

"Yes ma'am but I will be sad ma'am and I will miss you," she replied sadly.

"Don't worry. I'm sure we will meet again," I told her.

"Ma'am, what do you like to order?" Dyna asked me. I was transported back from my thoughts of the past to the restaurant in the present.

"Whatever you order, that's also my order," I answered.

During that dinner, I was so happy to learn that Dyna had completed a two-year degree in Information Technology and that she had an opportunity to work in Canada with her twin sister Dona. There she met her Canadian boyfriend who she plans to marry in June.

While we were dining, her boyfriend arrived and was introduced to me. Her boyfriend was so proud of Dyna because she was so fluent in English. They invited me to attend their wedding. I was touched. Before we left the restaurant, Dyna handed over a small card and told me to open it when I reached home.

On my way home, I couldn't contain my feelings of gladness and joy. Imagine my former student, Dyna—the slow reader in high school, now an accomplished professional! I realized that through my efforts and my patience in teaching Dyna, I somehow contributed to her success.

That night, as I sat down to prepare yet another lesson for my students, I opened the card that Dyna gave. I was touched by the message:

> To my dear teacher,
> Thank you very much for what you had done for me.
> Without you during my high school days
> I will not be a successful person now.
> What you had done for me is priceless
> I don't know what I can give you in return.
> Nothing I can pay you my dear teacher
> I just want to say thank you very much
> I can't forget you. You're one in a million
> I love you.
>
> *Love, Dyna*

At that moment, I fully understood the role God wanted me to play in this world. If I were born again and had another chance to choose my profession, I would still choose teaching. There are still many like Dyna who I can help. There are still more like her that I can guide to help them find their way to success.

Never Give Up on Geoffrey

LITO A. PALOMAR
Antipolo National High School, Antipolo City

It all started with an assignment. I was then a substitute teacher for Mrs. Gatlabayan who at that time had filed for a two-month sick leave. Geoffrey, a freshman student from Section 33, was very angry and started cursing his group leader for giving him a "no assignment" mark on that day.

"Sir, it is not my fault that the Merriam-Webster Dictionary failed to include the antonym of *love* in the reference!" he explained. "Why should she give me a *no assignment* mark then?" he added with strong sarcasm. His classmate told me that Geoffrey and his girlfriend, Ethel, also a classmate, had a big fight before my session.

"Geoffrey," I said in a soft tone. "You won't find the antonym of any word in a dictionary. Why not try a thesaurus?" Geoffrey frowned. He appeared puzzled about the word "thesaurus," which I bet was a word he hasn't encountered before. I excused him from his assignment that day and gave him another assignment instead.

"Very well then, I'll give you another chance. This time it is a special assignment. This is just yours, okay?" I felt his interest increase. He seemed excited with a new opportunity to do a special assignment. "Find the antonym of the word *life*. Go to the library and this time, use a thesaurus." Geoffrey immediately took a pen and wrote the word on his palm. But before he rushed to the school library, I said, "By the way, the antonym of *love* is *hate*." The boy nodded.

I remember the first day I met Geoffrey. He was wearing an old polo shirt with a rust-stained collar, a torn right sleeve, and some missing buttons. His faded brown trousers were patched with stickers to cover slits and holes. If there was anything pleasant in that set of uniform he wore regularly, that would be his new pair of socks, which was a gift from his mother when he graduated from grade school. "It's all that his mother can afford for his graduation," his best friend told me.

Geoffrey was so proud of this new pair of socks that he would always remove his shoes inside the classroom and roam around to show off his clean white socks. I remember watching him slide from one row to another with those socks on. Sometimes he would raise his feet and force his smaller classmates to smell the new socks. Once, he volunteered to erase the blackboard using his socks. In one incident, Geoffrey got into a fight with a classmate who tried to pull his socks off his feet. Geoffrey's socks had become a regular part of my daily life with Section Thirty-three.

Geoffrey's uncombed hair, yellowish teeth, and untrimmed fingernails were proof of poor personal hygiene. His classmates and other teachers would often say that he was a total disaster—physically, socially, and intellectually. But I did not agree. I had a strange sense, a gut feeling, that Geoffrey was just a troubled boy.

The next morning, Geoffrey came to class again without having done his homework assignment. "There is no available thesaurus in the library," Geoffrey explained.

"Are you sure? You know that the library will never run out of references, right?" I asked.

Scratching his head, he said, "I'm so sorry sir. I don't want go to the library, that's why." I thought he was just afraid of the librarian. To my surprise, he admitted that he was afraid of the thesaurus, thinking that the thesaurus was a beast that would eat him alive. I burst into laughter.

"A thesaurus is a book, Geoffrey. It is a reference for antonyms and synonyms of words," I explained. Realizing his misconception of the word "thesaurus," he smiled and then apologized. "Now for your new assignment—I want you to find the antonym of the word *pride*," I said.

"Yes sir, right away sir!" Geoffrey exclaimed.

"And by the way Geoffrey," I added. "The antonym of *life* is *death*." And the boy just nodded.

I once read in Geoffrey's journal that he considered suicide to get away from his family's problems. Poor Geoffrey, I thought. He worried too much about escaping from these problems while ignoring the fact that staying out of focus from his studies would only make his situation worse. I had always wanted to confront him about this and be a shoulder to lean on, but I realized that I needed more time to earn his trust.

The next morning, I was excited to find out how Geoffrey dealt with that vicious thesaurus beast. But to my disappointment, Geoffrey did not go to school. I waited the whole day hoping that Geoffrey would see me and turn in his assignment. Geoffrey did not go to school for three straight days.

Monday morning came. Geoffrey was there in my Section 33 class, ready to have his homework checked. I couldn't hide my excitement. "Sir, the antonym of *pride* is *humility*," Geoffrey declared.

"You are correct, Geoffrey. That is very good!" I replied. Then I told him that I would give him a perfect score for completing his assignment that day. In my excitement, I had forgotten to ask why he was absent for three days. Geoffrey smiled at me and asked for another assignment, so he could get a perfect score everyday.

I realized then that I should never give up on Geoffrey. I said, "Very well. I want you to find the antonym of the word *optimism*. Hope I'll see you tomorrow, okay?"

"Don't worry boss, I will see you tomorrow," Geoffrey answered.

The next morning, Geoffrey presented his assignment. Again he was correct in stating that the opposite of *optimism* is *pessimism*. I wasn't surprised that Geoffrey was able to complete his assignment again. What caught my attention that day was that Geoffrey was not wearing his new pair of socks.

In the days that followed, Geoffrey became more and more cheerful and active in class recitations, especially if the topic was vocabulary. Everyday his performance improved. Everyday I observed his confidence grow. But everyday, he did not wear the new pair of socks he was always proud of.

One morning, I asked him why he didn't wear his socks. He replied, "Sir, why not go to the library and find the synonym of the word *importance* in the thesaurus?" And so I did. Even if I did know the answer, I thought it best to visit the school library.

"Ma'am, may I see the thesaurus?" I asked the librarian.

"There is no available thesaurus at the moment, sir," the librarian replied. "There is a group of students who always borrows the thesaurus for their assignments. One boy always waits for them to return the reference, but he is still unable to borrow the book."

"Is this boy Geoffrey Miranda?" I asked the librarian.

"Yes sir," the librarian replied. I thought to myself—if Geoffrey couldn't borrow a thesaurus at the library, how was he able to complete his assignments? Where does he get all his answers?

The next morning I asked Geoffrey how he was able to do his homework assignments. Geoffrey replied, "Sir, I have never been absent in school. I may not be the brightest student in your class but I make it a point not to be absent from class."

Geoffrey continued: "The reason why I did not go to class for three days was because I was busy looking for someone who would trade his thesaurus for my new pair of socks. And I did find one! Now I have my own thesaurus I can use for all my assignments."

I was speechless and teary-eyed. "Why would you trade your socks? They're gifts from your mother," I asked him.

"Remember? I asked you to find the synonym of the word *importance?* I wanted you to know that no matter how important those socks are to me, it is more valuable to finish my studies. I can only do that if I have my own reference book. I can do it even without a new pair of socks," he explained.

At that moment, I realized that I was looking at a boy waiting to be trusted and affirmed. Contrary to what most teachers and students thought, Geoffrey was not a hopeless boy after all. Making him check the thesaurus everyday taught him the value of initiative, determination, and discipline.

At the end of that school year, I received the following letter from Geoffrey:

Dear Sir Palomar,

Thank you sir for changing me. Trading my socks for a thesaurus was one of the hardest decisions I had ever made. But it was all worth it. More than the synonyms and antonyms of words, my thesaurus taught me a lot of lessons about life.

The antonym of love *is* greed *and not* hate. *Because that very day when Ethel and I parted ways, it was the same moment I realized that keeping her beside me and taking her away from her friends is but pure greed. I love her. I really do. That is why I set her free.*

You were wrong when you said that the opposite of life is death. I have realized that the antonym of life *is* living *and not* death. *I once tried to commit suicide due to a family problem but I realized that God gave me life and I have to live it. Life not lived to the fullest is the same as death gained without effort.*

The antonym of pride *is* self-respect *and not* humility. *When people become so proud of what they have received or what they have achieved, they tend to abuse themselves and they lose self-respect. I began respecting myself the moment I gave up on my pride.*

Lastly, let me correct you by saying that the antonym of optimism *is* not *pessimism* but *hope. Optimism is just sitting down and thinking positively that everything falls into place. Hope is not. Hope is more than just positive thinking. Hope is doing something, a solid and concrete action to achieve your goal. I was tired of just thinking positively about passing in your subject without doing anything, I was wrong. I passed in your subject because I did something about it.*

Thank you very much sir and I will never regret trading my socks for these wonderful lessons in life that you and my old thesaurus I once called "beast" and "vicious" have taught me.

Sincerely,
Geoffrey

Indeed, as an educator I have come to realize that teaching is more about passion than profession. I have tried other jobs before—as sales representative, customer-relations executive, account manager for an electric company, agent for an international airline, and a hotel and car reservation specialist. All were financially rewarding, but never once did these jobs bring me exceptional satisfaction—the satisfaction of the heart and definition of the soul.

They say no two stories are the same. Mine is just one story among a thousand other inspiring stories from teachers. Who would have known that it would take just one old and torn thesaurus to change two lives—mine and Geoffrey's? Who would have thought that it would take only one troubled boy to make me find true meaning in my work place?

Indeed, we cannot change the world overnight. We as teachers should not only strive to change the world. We should *be the change*. Imagine what kind of world it would be if each teacher would nurture at least one Geoffrey in his classroom.